D1556320

An Unexpected Journey:

To Road to Power and Wisdom in Divorced Co-Parenting

Alisa Jaffe Holleron

Live Oak Publishing

Live Oak Publishing
5011 Golden Foothill Parkway, Suite 6
El Dorado Hills, CA 95762

ISBN-13: 978-0615704227
ISBN-10: 0615704220
Library of Congress Control Number: 2012952444

"Hatred never ceases by hatred, but by love alone is healed.
This is an ancient and eternal law."

The Buddha

"It may be when we no longer know what to do,
we have come to our real work,
and that when we no longer know which way to go,
we have begun our real journey."

Wendell Berry

Gratitude

I am grateful for many dear friends and colleagues who have been a great source of encouragement and help.

I am grateful for wise teachers whose words and ways of being have spoken to my mind and heart.

I am grateful for the many divorced co-parents who have entrusted me with their stories and struggles. I am touched by their courage, openness and willingness to grow, and appreciate what they have taught me.

I am grateful for my parents who have always loved me and believed in me, and my sons whose creativity, intelligence and ability to think out of the box have challenged me and inspired me.

I am grateful for my husband who is "there" in so many ways, loving and supporting me.

Table of Contents

Introduction

In the co-parenting classes I have taught over the years, most of the participants were engaged in high conflict divorce situations and were ordered by the Court to participate. Initially, I used a curriculum that focused on communication skills, cooperation and the effects of conflict on children. After quickly learning how difficult it was to teach people to communicate and cooperate when tensions were high, I became determined to find ideas and methods that would be more helpful. Undeniably, the participants in the classes were in a great deal of pain. Having been through a difficult divorce some years before, I understood and felt for that pain. I wanted to be able to contribute something practical that would lessen the pain and make their lives better.

Over time, I have made some discoveries that have helped me work with divorced parents more effectively. The most important one is that you can teach communication skills to people, but when they are in emotionally reactive states, they will not be able to use them. Divorce that involves children stirs up our deepest feelings about security, family and self-worth. When our sense of security, our relationship with our children or our self-worth is threatened in some way, we become emotionally reactive. When we are in an emotionally reactive state of mind, when we are angry, frustrated, fearful, anxious or resentful -- or all of the above-- we are unable to be rational and logical. One of my favorite sayings is: **You cannot talk to emotions with logic.** Telling a person when she is in the throes of intense emotion to communicate nicely is an exercise in ridiculousness.

Another discovery I made is that the word "co-parenting" can be a detriment. It is a mushy and loving word, but people in these situations are not feeling mushy and loving. I often heard comments such as: "It is absurd to think that we are 'co-parenting'-- my ex is a bully, and has no interest in compromising and communicating. How do you co-parent with someone who has no interest in co-parenting?" Or: "This class makes me feel guilty, because it stresses me out that I am hurting my children if I don't adopt these ideas. As much as I try, I can't seem to use these ideas in my real life, and I walk away feeling like I've failed and I'm a terrible parent." Or my favorite: "Whoever wrote the co-parenting curriculum never met my ex-husband/wife!"

The problem with the word "co-parenting" is that it implies that the **two** people in the relationship should be able to parent together, that they should be able to cooperate and communicate, and that if they can't, they are hurting their children. The problem with this, and the most frequent complaint I've heard about this approach, is that even if **your** intention is to communicate effectively, you cannot **make the other person do it.** People get frustrated because they feel like they are trying, but they can't control what their "co-parent" does. When you hold out hope that your ex will "co-parent" with you, and then she doesn't, it actually makes things worse. (Please note that I will be alternating between "he" and "she" when referring to co-parents.)

Here's another discovery I've made: It is not true that you **both** have to be on board in order to make things better. I believe that if you are in a significant amount of conflict with your ex, and feel as though you can't communicate with him, you can still significantly improve the situation just by the changes that you make within yourself.

So this book is focused on **YOU** – helping you gain power and wisdom. In these situations, people feel and act out of powerlessness. We feel as though we are losing control over the things most deeply important to us-- our children and our sense of security. When we feel powerless, we tend to behave in irrational and desperate ways, further diffusing our power. We create an emotional "loop" that is very difficult to disengage from.

What I have come to then, is that what people need in these situations is not to be told what they have to give up, or how they should be nicer and more compromising. Conversely, they need to know how to step into their power. This book is going to teach you to be powerful because children do better when their parents are confident, secure and in control of themselves. In divorce situations, children already feel insecure as a result of the changes and disruptions in their family. When parents act out of control and desperate it only makes matters worse.

Power, as I define it here, is all about being able to control our emotional reactivity so that we can be smart. True power and wisdom go hand in hand. When we can control our emotional reactivity, we can think clearly about what we are trying to accomplish and how to accomplish it. When we are being controlled by our emotional reactivity, we almost always work against what we really want. **Power is more about being in control of ourselves than being in control of others**. We think of power as being aggressive, but, in fact, aggression is often powerless, because it comes out of an emotionally reactive, desperate place.

True power is about effectiveness. It is about being able to see clearly what we want and how to go about getting it. Power can look very quiet. Power is a feeling of knowing, of feeling strong within ourselves. It is the feeling of being in control of ourselves and not at the mercy of others. Power is the ability to stand our ground like the oak tree that sways in the wind but doesn't get blown over.

Chapter 1
An Unexpected Journey

When one door of happiness closes, another opens; but often we look so long at the closed door that we do not see the one which has been opened for us.
Helen Keller

When clients tell me they are falling apart, I often say "Great!" If we're falling apart, we have the opportunity to put ourselves back together in a new and better way. Difficult times give us the opportunity to recreate our lives. If we find ourselves in this place, it is because there is some significant way that our lives aren't working, or at least as well as they could be. Sometimes we seem to need dramatic events, like divorce or separation, to propel us into a better place.

I'm not suggesting that we should feel happy about how difficult our lives are. Rather, I am suggesting that we have two choices. We can see ourselves as victims, or we can see ourselves as having an opportunity. Which do you choose?

What do we want to create?

We have the opportunity right now to start creating a better, more fulfilling life for ourselves and our children. In order to create the life we want to have, it is imperative that we know what we're trying to create. If we don't know what we are aiming toward, it is unlikely that we will get there. It would be like deciding that we want to go on a road trip to a beautiful destination but not really being clear about what the destination is, not taking a road map or a GPS and just trusting that we are going to get there if we keep driving along. We might decide to turn right or left because that's what all the other people are doing or because one road looks more appealing or easier in the moment. Many people live their lives like this, bumbling along with no real destination in mind.

Step one in this journey is clearly defining what we want. Because we are all different, we want different things, but there are some things everyone wants. Most of us want to be happy and feel a sense of fulfillment in our lives. We want to feel as though our lives have some value and are enjoyable. As parents, the happiness and success of our children is generally closely tied to our own happiness. It is difficult to feel happy or fulfilled if our children are suffering or miserable.

When we think about happiness, we tend to think about the circumstances that will make us happy. For instance, we may believe that if we have a good spouse, a good job and two kids, we will be happy. But we also know that getting the things we want doesn't automatically guarantee happiness. Happiness is about how we feel, regardless of the circumstances. We can be very happy sharing a meal of peanut butter and jelly sandwiches with our children. We can be very unhappy having a meal at a gourmet restaurant. We can be happy walking our children to school on a rainy day, and we can be unhappy at Disneyland on a beautiful day. Happiness often has little to do with what we have and what we are doing, and everything to do with our state of mind.

Our children's states of mind largely mirror our own. We are the most important role models in their lives. If we are often in states of fear, resentment, anger and frustration, our children will "learn" these states from us. Therefore, if we want our children to be happy and stable, our best bet is to be happy ourselves. "The most important thing that parents need to understand is that the brain of their child will become exactly what the child was exposed to," states Bruce Perry, child psychiatrist and internationally recognized authority on childhood trauma, in an interview with Patricia Gras on "Living Smart." "If you want your child to be kind then you have to be kind to the child. If you want your child to be good at self-regulation and not lose their temper, you have to not lose your temper....It's really important for parents to understand that their internal state, whether it's calm or whether it's alert engagement or whether it's frustration and anger, whether it's sadness or depression, the baby [child] absorbs these internal states." (http://www.youtube.com/watch?v=vak-iDwZJY8).

I am not suggesting that we pretend we're happy or that we are damaging our child if we aren't happy all the time. I am suggesting that if we cultivate happiness, or peacefulness, or calm, we will help our children cultivate those qualities. In divorced co-parenting situations, we often get upset and wrapped up in worrying about certain things, such as how much time our child is spending with us, or if we will have enough money, or what our ex, or our ex's partner, is saying about us. These things matter little when it comes to the ultimate happiness and success of our children. What matters most is our state of mind.

Emotional reactivity

The stress of conflicted co-parenting situations tends to propel us into emotional reactivity—into states where we act predominantly out of negative emotions and not out of reason, rationality, logic or, most importantly, love. When we are angry, frustrated, anxious, scared or full of resentment, we rarely work toward what we really want. We can't see the big picture or the future, or be wise about what we are trying to create. In emotionally reactive states, we are overcome by an uncomfortable level of distress that compels us to want to take action RIGHT NOW.   We focus all of our energy on the event that triggered our emotional response and lose the ability to contemplate the impact of our actions on others or on future events. We become completely single-minded.

Emotional reactions are necessary and even lifesaving in certain threatening situations. We want to be emotionally reactive when a toddler runs toward a busy street. We want the world to collapse into the narrowness of the situation, and we want to focus all of our attention and energy on fixing it. We want to stop paying attention to everything else and put all of our energy toward catching the child before he gets to street. We don't want to waste any energy considering the options. That could be disastrous.

The problem is that the majority of times that we get triggered into emotional reactivity, we are not in that kind of extreme situation. We may feel threatened, but we are not truly in danger. Because we lose our ability to think things through and to contemplate the impact of our actions on others and on the future, and because we feel as though we have limited options, we wind up taking action that actually works against what we are trying to create.

In difficult divorced parenting situations we are especially susceptible to emotional reactivity because the stakes are so high. When we feel as though our children's wellbeing or our relationship with our children is being threatened, it is natural to get emotionally reactive. We barge forward without forethought or caution. Unfortunately, actions that result from anger, fear or resentment are often acts of foolishness because ultimately they do not get us what we want.

For example, since the ability to be in healthy relationships is one of the most important determinants of happiness, our true desire is for our children to be in healthy relationships. Yet often we work against what we truly want by staying mired in anger, negativity or resentment toward our ex or continuing to engage in conflict with our ex.   We convince ourselves that the conflict we are engaged in with our ex or the negative feelings we harbor are not really affecting our children.

Children learn from us

Children learn about relationships from us. We may think that if we are nice to the cashier at the grocery store or to our friends, we are modeling how to get along with others. This is erroneous. In fact, how we are in relationship with our ex is one of the primary ways we teach our children about relationships. We might have the true desire of wanting our children to learn how to be in healthy relationships, but if we are engaged in a continuing conflict with our ex, if we are feeling resentful, negative or angry toward our ex, we are teaching our children how to stay engaged in conflict and stay steeped in anger, negativity and resentment.

Another way we work against our true desires is by "believing what we think" when we are in reactive states. In difficult divorce situations, it is not uncommon to stay in a prolonged state of emotional reactivity. One of the characteristics of emotional reactions, and the most damaging, is that we can't think of anyone but ourselves. This means we are not thinking about our children. We often **think** that we are acting in the best interest of our children, but when we are so narrowly focused on our own emotions, we cannot really consider theirs. This is one of the most dangerous parts of these situations. **It is easy to think that what WE need to make ourselves feel better is also what our children need.** Not being able to discern the difference between what we need and what our children need leads us to do things that actually work against our true desires.

A common example of this is for parents to think that their children should spend less time, or no time at all, with their other parent. This type of thinking stems from fear about how the other parent is parenting the child. We may believe that because we feel fearful or uncomfortable, it is in the best interest of the children to spend less or no time with their other parent. However, unless the child/ren is actually in some kind of danger, this is not true. Creating barriers to their relationship with their other parent, even if we think it is inferior to our relationship, does not benefit our children.

It takes a lot of wisdom to know the difference between what would **feel good** for us and what is **actually good** for our children. Wisdom means having the clarity and resolve to stay focused on helping our children grow up to be happy, self-assured, competent and fulfilled in life. Wisdom means being honest with ourselves about whether what we are doing is contributing to our children's well-being. We want our children to grow up to be happy, to enjoy their lives, to feel good about themselves, to know how to care for and love others, and to feel a sense of accomplishment and competency. Because we want these things, we can find the courage to let go of blame and anger. Because we love our children, we can do the hard work of turning toward ourselves and asking ourselves what **WE** can do to contribute to their wellbeing.

Grounded vs. Reactive Desires
To become wise and powerful, we must learn the difference between true or "grounded desires" and "reactive desires." A grounded desire comes from a deep knowing in our hearts. When we are focused on a grounded desire, we are in an open-hearted, calm, clear-headed and

compassionate frame of mind. A reactive desire comes from erroneous thoughts driven by reactive emotions. Reactive desires are the things that we want when we are acting out of our emotional reactivity; when we are collapsed into ourselves and our desires are coming out of fear, resentment, negativity, anger and hatefulness.

Examples of Grounded Desires:

I want to raise children that are well-adjusted and fulfilled in life.
I want to raise my children in a way that will enable them to be successful in life.
I want my life to feel peaceful and contented.
I want to feel fulfilled and secure.
I want my children to be safe.

Examples of Reactive Desires:

I want my children to know the truth about how bad their father is.
I want my child to have less time with my ex.
I want to show my ex how wrong she is.
I want to get revenge on my ex.
I want my children to hate my ex just like I do.
I want my ex to suffer.
I don't want my ex to win.

If we focus on reactive desires, we will create more powerlessness, negativity and unhappiness in our lives. If we focus on grounded desires, we will become more powerful, happy and positive. We will create what we want in our lives. The reason that we are powerful when we are in a grounded desire is that we are calm and grounded, and we are able to think straight and be smart. When we are in an emotional reaction, we are largely unable to engage the part of our brain that exercises judgment and rationality.

It is very difficult to turn away from reactive desires. It takes effort and practice. We can become very attached to our reactive desires. We can hang onto them like they are life jackets in a stormy sea. The problem is that they may feel like life jackets, but they keep us bobbing forever on the stormy sea. Is that how we want to live?

You are on an unexpected journey. It is not where you thought you would be. But you can learn to be happy and to help your child/ren be happy and successful. Be clear about where you are going and make a commitment to cultivating the skills and state of mind that insures you will get there.

"Be Careful What You Wish For"
(Based on a true story with names changed to protect privacy)

Tim tells the story like this: His wife Sarah suddenly announced that she was no longer happy and wanted a divorce. Totally blindsided, he felt his life turned upside down. He couldn't imagine divorcing and having his 10-year-old son and 8-year-old daughter go back and forth between two homes. Tim found himself obsessing about their new arrangement. The financial aspects felt overwhelming-- he made a lot more money than Sarah did and feared that between the divorce and child support, he'd be left with nothing. He was devastated—alternating between fear, sadness and anger. When he thinks back on it, he doesn't know how he made it through that first year.

At about the year mark, a new man arrived on the scene. Justin, Sarah's boyfriend, had a daughter very close in age to their daughter. Tim was amazed at how quickly this new relationship between Sarah and Justin developed. Within six months, the "new family" was living together, and within a year Sarah and Justin were married. Still reeling from the divorce, Tim felt like a zombie. Mostly he just muddled through, still struggling with moments, or even hours, of intense and sometimes debilitating emotions. Justin, on the other hand, was alive and energetic, excited about being a parent to two more kids. The two new step-sisters loved the new arrangement --after all, they now lived with their new best friend. Tim felt like Justin was trying to steal his kids away. When the kids talked about Justin or his daughter, or when Tim saw them with together, he felt physically ill. He didn't have the energy to compete.

Tim believed that Justin's positive attitude was just a façade and that below the surface he was conniving, manipulative and mean. He couldn't believe that Sarah and the kids had been taken in by this man. The anger and jealousy was so strong and painful that he could barely stand to be in his own skin. He was afraid that eventually his kids would want nothing to do with him. He saw nothing but loneliness and pain stretched out in front of him for many years.

Tim wished for Sarah to hurt as badly as he was. He wished that Sarah and Justin would start to fight. He wished that they would divorce. He wished that his kids would start to see how evil Justin was. He wished that his kids would go through their miserable adolescent years and turn on Justin the way only adolescents can do. He imagined that if the things he wished for came true, he would have the upper hand, and the kids would have him and only him for their father, and he would live happily ever after.

Ten years later, Tim says: "Be careful what you wish for."

All those things came true. Sarah and Justin got divorced. It was a bitter and ugly ending, and of course the kids were in the home enduring the hatred and bitterness that was hanging in the air between Justin and Sarah. "Justin doesn't talk to or see my kids now," Tim explained. "After a short honeymoon period, they did turn on him. They didn't like that he was trying to insert himself in their lives. They didn't like that he took over the discipline in the family. His dictatorial style was very different than mine, and they resented it. They would remind him loudly that he wasn't their father. He felt rejected by them and angry that they showed him no respect. He became very bitter, reminding Sarah often how miserable her kids were, often in front of them."

The years Sarah and Justin were together were not happy. "Is that what I wanted for my kids? Really?" asks Tim. "Sure, a part of me feels smug and superior. But really, is that what I wanted for my kids? To be in a household that wasn't really happy for all those years? I see now how hard it was for them, and how much it bogged them down and made them sad. Am I really happy that they ended a ten-year relationship with their step-dad and have nothing to show for it but bitterness? Did that benefit them somehow?

"Sometimes, now, I get angry at Justin. I get angry because he walked away from them, because he turned on them when they rejected him and wasn't man enough to not blame them, because he wanted too much from them and didn't give them enough. I am mad at him because half of the time for the years Justin and Sarah were together they lived in a home where there was conflict and negativity.

"Amazing," muses Tim. "I am mad at him for doing all the things that I wished for. Did my wishes play a part? I don't imagine that I am so powerful that I created these things because I wished for them, but is there a way my negativity contributed to the situation? If I had wished that things would go well, if I had understood that my negative desires were not in the best interest my kids, if I had known that my bond with my kids was too strong, and that Justin could never replace me, if I had somehow sent good wishes instead of bad, would that have helped?"

It certainly couldn't have hurt.

Exercises for Chapter 1

1. What specific things do you find yourself angry, frustrated or resentful about? How do these feelings have an effect on your child/ren?

2. List ten reactive desires that you have had, and ten grounded desires.

3. Choose the grounded desire that is most important to you. Write it down in large letters on a piece of paper and hang it on your refrigerator.

4. Throughout the course of your day, notice when you have a grounded desire and when you have a reactive desire. If you notice a reactive desire, try consciously to turn yourself away from it, and toward a grounded desire. What reactive and grounded desires did you notice? Were you able to turn toward grounded desires?

Chapter 2
Mindful Awareness is a Powerful Tool

Mindfulness is simply being aware of what is happening right now without wishing it were different; enjoying the pleasant without holding on when it changes (which it will); being with the unpleasant without fearing it will always be this way (which it won't).
James Baraz

Psychologists have learned in recent years that more than anything, in order to develop in a healthy manner, children need **attuned connected presence**. This means they need their parents and caregivers to be alert to their experience and feel connected to their experience. When I say "their experience," I mean what they are experiencing in the moment-- simply what they are feeling, sensing and thinking. It is impossible to be fully attuned and connected all of the time, but if we are concerned about raising healthy, well-adjusted children, it is imperative that we strive to be attuned to them as often as possible.

Let's think in a more detailed way what it means to be attuned and connected to our children. It means that we are paying close attention-- noticing the many things that give us information about what they are experiencing. We notice their body language, their facial expressions, what they are saying, what they are emoting, etc. We attempt to understand what it is like to be them and what it is like to see the world through their eyes. One of the most important things about this type of attention is that we are not **judging** their experience- we are just noticing it. Once we start judging it, we are not seeing it clearly any more. For instance, if a child is crying and we have the judgment "He should not be crying," we are no longer gathering information about it because we have already decided it's wrong and we are thinking about how to make it stop. We spend a lot of time trying to get children to do what we need them to do, and trying to get them to be what we think they should be, and not enough time just noticing who they are.

Emotional reactivity and attunement

When we are in emotionally reactive states, we cannot be attuned to our children. We focus all of our energy on the event that triggered our emotional response and lose the ability to contemplate the impact of our actions on others INCLUDING OUR CHILDREN. We become completely single-minded. We are focused on our own reactive desires, and are not attuned to anyone, INCLUDING and MOST IMPORTANTLY OUR CHILDREN.

It doesn't matter how much good stuff we buy our children or how many times we take them to Disneyland or how great we make their birthday party. If we are not attuned to them, we are not giving them what they need the most. If we stay in emotional reactivity, we are taking away precious attuned presence from our children.

When we are not attuned to our children it is impossible to know what they need. When we stay in emotionally reactive states we never really understand what our children need or what they really experience. We imagine that what WE need is what THEY need. **Mistaking our needs for our children's needs when we are in emotionally reactive states is the biggest and most harmful mistake we can make.**

The intention of my words is not to instill guilt about the mistakes we have already made. The intention is to wake us up. We all want to do what will contribute to our children's well-being. We never intend to hurt our children. But by staying unconscious, we can and do inadvertently hurt our children.

Being attuned to ourselves

We must learn how to get out of our own emotional reactivity so that we can become attuned to our children. **In order to be attuned to them, we first have to cultivate an acute awareness of our own experience.** It is amazing to realize that a majority of the time, we are on autopilot; we have very little idea of how we are feeling, what we are thinking or how we are experiencing the world in any given moment. When we are on autopilot, it is like we are being driven, instead of being the driver. We do not have the ability to be truly present with our children and we lose our ability to take control because some automatic state controls us. The automatic state is basically old unconscious habitual patterns of behavior and reactivity that have become deeply engrained in us.

Being in a reactive state prevents us from being present to our own experience. If we think about the times that we are triggered into negative states such as anger, frustration, anxiety, confusion or resentment, we realize that we are either obsessing about the past or the future. We are not "in the moment."

Mindfulness is a technique used to bring ourselves into the present so that we are not on autopilot. Jon Kabat-Zinn, professor of medicine emeritus and founding director of the Stress Reduction Clinic and the Center for Mindfulness in Medicine, Health Care, and Society at the University of Massachusetts Medical School, defines mindfulness as: **"Paying attention on purpose in the present moment as if your life depended on it, non-judgmentally."**
(Mindfulness for Beginners- Audio presentation- Sounds True, 2006)

When it comes to divorced co-parenting, there are two very important advantages to cultivating mindfulness:

1. It helps us stay in control of emotions that tend to create trouble for us.
2. It helps us be present with ourselves so that we can be present with our children.

Mindfulness is the deliberate attempt to pay attention to our present moment experience **without judgment.** It is like we have a very friendly and loving little scientist on our shoulder saying "Hmm, now I am feeling angry, and now I am noticing that I am feeling anxiety in the pit of my stomach." What we are paying attention to in the moment are the following: feelings, thoughts and bodily sensations.

Mindfulness directions
In order to become mindful, the first thing you do is notice that you are not being mindful.
When you take notice of that, bring yourself to mindfulness by noticing your breath. Focusing on your breathing brings you solidly into the present moment and has the added benefit of calming you down. Notice yourself breathing in and notice yourself breathing out. Do not try to control your breath, simply notice it. Notice if it is shallow or deep. Notice where your breath goes. Notice it going in through your nose and into your lungs and then perhaps down into your stomach.

Next, take notice of how you are feeling in your body. Pay attention to your bodily sensations. Are you tense? Where? Do you feel any pain? Where? What does the pain or tension feel like? Notice how you are feeling emotionally. Are you angry, sad, anxious, resentful? Are your emotions connected to your bodily sensations?

Now, notice what kinds of thoughts you are thinking. Watch the thoughts come and go. Notice if you are judging yourself and the feelings and thoughts that you are having. You may want to try labeling the things you notice about your present moment experience. For instance, if you feel angry, you may want to think to yourself: "anger, anger, anger." Or if your angry thoughts are out of control, you may want to think to yourself: "angry thoughts, angry thoughts."

When you are attempting to be mindful, you will inevitably drift out of mindfulness. That is natural and normal. When you notice that you are no longer being mindful, simply bring yourself gently back to mindfulness by refocusing on your breath.

Non-judgment
We tend to harshly judge ourselves a lot. It is actually very difficult to simply observe ourselves without judgment. We think we shouldn't feel certain ways or do certain things, and then we beat ourselves up for how we feel or what we do. Notice the judgments you make about yourself from a more compassionate point of view. In other words, notice that you are judging yourself, and notice that the part of you that is noticing that fact is not judging. It is important to find a part of yourself that is simply observing and noticing, not judging. That part of you is not reactive, and that is the part you want to learn to step into more and more.

When we are able to notice how we are feeling in the moment, we have more control over whether we are going to act out of that feeling. For instance, if we are aware that we are angry, and noticing our anger, we are probably in control enough to not unthinkingly lash out. This is very different than being consumed by our anger and acting out of it without awareness. When we are in an emotional reaction, the part of our brain that has the ability to reason, be rational and exercise judgment is basically impaired. When we attempt to bring ourselves into mindfulness, we engage those parts of our brain. The more we can be mindful and not act out when we are in a negative emotional state, the more we will be able to exercise good judgment and not behave in a way that we will later regret. It may not be easy, but **IT IS** possible!

Remember that being mindful helps us be attuned to ourselves, and when we are attuned to ourselves we can become attuned to our children. **THE MOST IMPORTANT THING WE CAN DO**

16

FOR OUR CHILDREN IS GIVE THEM OUR FULL ATTENTION! Even if the amount of time that we have with them is small, the time that we have with them can be powerful if we are attuned to them. If we waste the time we have with them being mad at our ex, we are doing our children a disservice. We must not fool ourselves into thinking that the time we spend obsessing about our ex is somehow benefitting our children. *It isn't.*

Mindfulness meditation

Mindfulness is a state of mind that is cultivated in the moment. Mindfulness meditation is a practice that helps us cultivate mindfulness so that we will be more skilled in it during our everyday life. The more skilled we become, the more we will be able to access mindfulness during the difficult moments of our lives.

Mindfulness meditation has become accepted in the psychological world as an effective tool for working with many difficult states of mind, including anxiety and depression. The explanation of mindfulness given here is brief, but I strongly encourage you to learn more, and to utilize books and CDs about mindfulness. Especially useful are CDs that include guided meditation. Several have been listed at the end of this chapter.

Being mindful and being attuned to our children takes practice. Let's be kind to ourselves if we cannot do it all the time, or even as much as we would like. If we can do it a little more than we did it yesterday, that is a **great thing**!

Exercises for Chapter 2

1. For ten minutes once a day, sit quietly, close your eyes and be mindful. Follow the mindfulness directions described. Describe what that experience was like.

2. During the course of your day, when you feel yourself getting angry or frustrated, take 10 deep breaths. Notice yourself breathing, and notice where in your body you feel the anger. Notice what your anger or frustration feels like in your body. Describe that experience.

3. Once a day, make an effort to be fully attuned to your child/ren. Take 10 deep breaths and then just be with them. Try to "feel into" their experience. Refrain from trying to make something happen. Simply enjoy being with them. What was that experience like?

Resources

Kabat-Zinn, Jon, Mindfulness for Beginners, (Audio CD) Sounds True, Incorporated; Unabridged edition (June 1, 2006)

Kabat-Zinn, Jon, Guided Mindfulness Meditation Series 1, (Audio CD), Sounds True, Unabridged edition (September 1, 2005)

Kabat-Zinn, Jon, Mindfulness for Beginners: Reclaiming the Present Moment—and Your Life, (Hardcover Book), Sounds True; Har/Com edition (December 28, 2011)

Kornfield, Jack , Meditation for Beginners: 10th-Anniversary Edition, (Abridged Audiobook) (Audio CD), Sounds True, Incorporated; 1 edition (June 28, 2010)

Siegel, Ronald D., The Mindfulness Solutions: Everyday Practices for Everyday Problems, The Guilford Press; 1 edition (November 9, 2009)

Chapter 3
Is What I Believe Really True?

Don't believe everything you think.
Unknown

When we are in emotionally reactive states (such as feeling anger, frustration, anxiety, fear or resentment), we are rarely working toward what we really want. We actually can't see the big picture or the future, or be wise about what we are trying to create. **In emotionally reactive states, we are overcome by an uncomfortable level of distress that compels us to want to take action RIGHT NOW.** We focus all of our energy on the event that triggered our emotional response and lose the ability to contemplate the impact of our actions on others or on future events. We become completely single-minded.

As we discussed in the Chapter 1, it is important to clearly understand the difference between grounded and reactive desires. This is particularly critical for divorced co-parenting because in emotionally reactive states, what we are really trying to do is relieve our discomfort. But as we try to accomplish that, we often work against our own goals, and against what is best for our children.

It is important to look at our misunderstandings and mistakes, and be honest with ourselves about what we are doing and why. In this chapter we will look at some common erroneous ideas held by parents in difficult co-parenting situations.

Error 1:
It is important to inform children about the specifics of what has happened in the parents' relationship. They are confused and need to know details so they can make sense of things.

Why this is an error:
Children do not see or understand the world the way we do. Even teenagers, who can look and act like adults, are not fully formed adults. It is confusing and upsetting to be told about these dynamics because it puts them in the position of taking sides, whether or not that is the intention. And feeling the need to choose a side is extremely detrimental to children of any age.
Whose need is this?
When we are talking to a child about adult matters, it is usually because we are hoping the child will side with us, or at least not blame us.

What do children really need?

They need to know that they are safe, secure and loved, and they need to know that we know they are distressed. When they ask questions like "Why did you and Daddy get divorced?" they are not looking for the answer that a friend would be looking for. Underlying every one of these kinds of questions is the need to know that they are going to be safe, secure and loved. We need to answer those kinds of questions with these things in mind. We need to let them know we understand how they feel and that their feelings are normal, and try to elicit what is REALLY bothering them. For instance, "I know it is hard and sad for you that we got divorced, but we both love you and that's what's most important to us. Is there anything you're worried about?" Respect the fact that they are "half" the other parent. If we try to convince our children that the other parent is bad, it will affect how they feel about themselves.

Therefore:

Don't involve them in discussions about adult relationship matters.

Don't try to talk them out of how they are feeling.

Don't speak negatively about the other parent.

Error 2:

Children aren't really affected by the conflict their parents are in. They don't pay much attention. They don't look upset. Besides, we don't say anything in front of the kids so they don't really know what's going on.

Why this is an error:

Kids are keenly aware of the conflict whether they show it or not. Because each parent is extremely important to a child and to a child's feeling of security, having parents in conflict is very frightening. It is like the ground they are standing on is shaky. The conflict can be deeply disturbing because it makes them fearful about their security and the impact the conflict will have on their lives. Fear is expressed in many different ways, and therefore it might be easy to miss the signs.

Whose need is this?

It is difficult and painful to be honest with ourselves about how our actions hurt our children. Convincing ourselves that they are not really affected keeps us from feeling the difficult feelings.

What do children really need?

They need you to learn to reduce or eliminate the conflict.

Therefore:

Never underestimate what your child/ren picks up.

Be aware of the conflict, and remind yourself that it is very hard on them.

Don't fool yourself.

Be honest with yourself about how you contribute to the conflict.

Be courageous and do the hard work to learn how to eliminate or greatly reduce the conflict.

Error 3:
Talking negatively about the other parent is OK because kids need to know the truth.

Why this is an error:
A child feels loyal to both parents. When we disparage the other parent, it makes children feel as though they have to take a side, which is terrible, confusing and frightening for them. Children ultimately figure out for themselves what their parents' strengths or weaknesses are and don't need our input. If we talk negatively about the other parent, we pull the child into the conflict. As noted before, conflict is very hard on children. If children are pulled into the conflict, it is even more frightening for them, because they feel like it is their job to make things better. It is terrifying for children to feel like they are somehow expected to make things better, because they know they are not equipped to do so.

Whose need is this?
If we are talking to children negatively about the other parent, it is because we are trying to win the children over to our side. If we deny this, we are fooling ourselves.

What do children really need?
They need to be kept out of the conflict. On a deep level, a child feels like he is "half" of each of his parents. If we convince him that his other parent is bad, what does this mean about him? If their other parent is truly bad, he needs help making sense of that parent in a compassionate way because staying in the same angry, resentful place that we are in will not serve him in the long run.

Therefore:
Do not talk negatively about the other parent to your child/ren.

Cultivate a compassionate understanding of the other parent's distress.

Do not use the excuse that your ex does it so you can too.

Take the high road.

Error 4:
My child/ren know the divorce is not their fault, and they don't feel responsible for it.

Why this is an error:
Children feel responsible for things because they have an egocentric view of the world. They do not understand marital love, marital discord or adult issues in general, so they try to make sense of it through the lens that they have available at their stage of development. If there is conflict,

and they know that the conflict has to do with them, they naturally think they are responsible for it. Even though the separation or divorce likely had nothing to do with the children, the conflict after the separation often focuses on issues about the children, so it can easily feel to them like they are to blame.

Whose need is this?

Again, it is painful for us to feel the effects the separation or divorce have on our children and it is easy to convince ourselves that our children are not feeling the effects.

What do children really need?

They need us to reduce the conflict so that it doesn't feel like we are fighting over them. If it feels like we are fighting over them, they will feel like they are responsible.

Therefore:

Be conscious of how they are put in the middle, even subtly, and don't do it.

Error 5:

It is OK to pass messages verbally or in writing through the child.

Why this is an error:

Being put in the middle is very difficult for children. It might seem benign to us but asking them to deliver messages is sending them the message that we and our ex can't communicate with each other. This is very unsettling for children and makes them feel like it is their job to mediate. It is extremely stressful for a child to be in the position of mediator between two adults. In essence, we are asking them to be more skilled communicators than we are.

Whose need this is?

Because we can be frustrated and confused about how communicate, it is easy to use our children as a go-between.

What do children really need?

Children need to feel like they are not being fought over. When we put them in the middle of conflict, they feel fought over. They need to be kids. They don't need to be mediators between their parents.

Therefore:

Don't send messages, either verbally or in writing, with your child/ren.

Error 6:

It is fine to make my child/ren keep the belongings that I bought at my house because I bought the belonging for them and it's not fair that they use it at the other house. Besides, I don't trust the other parent to care for the belonging the way I would expect it to be cared for at my house.

Why this is an error:

The experience of divorce can make children feel like they are split in two. Having two homes, two sets of rules, two parents, two everything, can be very hard on children. Can you imagine having two homes that you move back and forth between, not because you want to, but because you have to? Because we are divorced or separated, we cannot avoid this reality. We can, however, avoid contributing to this split-in-two feeling.

Whose need this is:

It is understandable that we want to see the clothes or toys we buy being used at our home. It is also understandable that we may fear that something will be broken or ruined, especially if that has happened in the past. Distress about these things can override our ability to see how it is affecting our children.

What do children really need?

Children need to feel whole. The situation they are in inherently makes them feel split. They need for us to do whatever we can to not contribute to the feeling of being "split in two."

Therefore:

Be conscious of how it feels for children to be "split in two."

Allow them to feel ownership of their own belongings.

Don't attach their belongings to one parent or the other.

Error 7:

Whenever my child/ren comes back after their time with the other parent they are in a bad mood and exhibit difficult behavior. This is because they are unhappy at the other home, or because the rules are different there than they are here. I have to undo all the damage that was done over there. Therefore, it is clear that my ex is not parenting adequately. Someone needs to make him parent better, or the children need to spend less time there.

Why this is an error:

Transitions are very hard for children. It is difficult to go from one environment to another. These transitions cause distress, and there are many different ways that children express distress. Acting out, withdrawing, throwing tantrums, expressing anger in a disrespectful way—these are all ways that distress is expressed.

Whose need is this?

Because we are already upset about the other parent, it is easy to conclude that the other parent is to blame for this behavior. When children are distressed, it is distressing to us. When we get distressed or feel like we don't know how to remedy the situation, it can be a natural reaction to want to blame someone.

What do children really need?

Children need to be understood and have a healthy way to express their feelings.

Therefore:

If your child/ren seem unhappy or behave badly when they come home from their other parent's home, or if they don't want to go to the other parent's home, don't immediately assume that their other parent is doing something wrong or that it's a bad idea for them to go there.

Work at cultivating an understanding of how difficult the transitions are.

Give your child/ren the opportunity to "chill out" and try not to take their behavior personally. Expecting that they are going to be distressed when they come back to you will help you avoid getting triggered by their behavior.

Error 8:

I will not have compassion for my ex because doing so would send the message to my child/ren that I am condoning my ex's behavior. I want my child/ren to know that the way my ex behaves is bad. Staying angry with my ex will communicate that to my child/ren.

Why this is an error:

Staying angry or resentful does not help children. Cultivating compassion does not mean that we have to love the other parent, approve of him, or be passive or not fight for things that we know (from a grounded place) are in our children's best interest. It does mean that we can develop some kind of understanding about why the other parent behaves the way she does. When we understand that people behave badly when they are distressed, we can have compassion for their distress. (This will be addressed more fully later.)

Whose need is this?

We can stay mired in anger and resentment, refusing to work toward cultivating compassion, because we think it will send the wrong message to our children. In addition, cultivating compassion is very hard emotional work. It takes a great deal of courage and an ability to look at ourselves honestly.

What do children really need?

Children will benefit immensely if we cultivate compassion for our ex. This does not mean that we will lie down, give up or give in. It simply means that we will cultivate an understanding of why our ex behaves the way he does. If our ex behaves badly, our children will need to make sense of it as well. When we cultivate compassion for our ex, it will help our children do so. As much as we think we might want our children to be angry with their other parent as well, this will not serve them emotionally. Learning to cultivate compassion for others contributes to emotional stability and happiness.

Therefore:

Difficult as it is when struggling with the kinds of emotions you likely struggle with, stay open to the idea that cultivating compassion for your ex will benefit your child/ren and benefit you. Consider that cultivating compassion for your ex will actually make you and your child/ren happier.

Exercises for Chapter 3

1. Read each error carefully. Find your courage and be honest. Put an "x" next to the ones that you have done or continue to do.

2. For the errors that you put an "x" next to, imagine being your child/ren. From their point of view, write a paragraph about what it feels like to them when you think or behave in the way that is described.

Chapter 4
If You Act Out of Fear, You Create What You Are Afraid Of

We gain strength, and courage, and confidence by each
experience in which we really stop to look fear in the face.
Eleanor Roosevelt

Internal experience is the stuff that happens **inside** of us. These experiences include our emotions, our thoughts and our physical sensations. **External experiences** are all the things that happen **outside** of us; that is, all the things that people say and do, the events that happen, the weather, the news, etc. External experiences "trigger" internal experiences. For example, when our ex says, "I'm going to file for custody and I'm going to win," it triggers the internal experience of fear, anger and hatefulness. In other words, we get triggered into an emotionally reactive state.

Remember that when we get into a state of emotional reactivity, **we are overcome by an intensely energetic uncomfortable level of distress that compels us to do something RIGHT NOW.** There are several things that are good about this state. First, it forces us to pay attention to the fact that something isn't right and that we may need to take action. Also, this state has a lot of energy in it, and energy directed productively is powerful.

However, when we stay in an emotionally reactive state and are not truly in a state of danger, we severely limit our ability to be smart and do things that will ultimately serve ourselves and our children. We are powerless because actions that come from negative emotions, such as anger, frustration and resentment, almost always lack power. These emotions may feel powerful because they have a lot of energy, but when they are not connected firmly to reason, rationality and judgment, they are like toddlers throwing a tantrum-- pure energy, no wisdom.

In order to learn how to avoid emotional triggers, or how to get ourselves out of an emotional reaction if we do get triggered, we have to understand the dynamics of emotional reactions, or how emotional reactions happen. One of the characteristics is that they happen very quickly and a lot happens in a very short period of time. In order to understand what's happening, we need to slow it down and look at it as if under a microscope.

The Power Suckers

There is a cluster of emotions that are problematic. These are: frustration, anger, resentment, hatefulness, exasperation and anxiety. When we get "triggered" we rarely feel one pure emotion; rather we feel some combination of the above. I call this cluster of emotions "The Power-Suckers" because, when they take over, they suck the power out of us. When the Power-Suckers are in control we have energy, but we must not trick ourselves into thinking that we are powerful. The energy is often very poorly directed and therefore diffused, wasted, dissipated, lost. We either stay stuck in these buzzing power-sucking emotions, or they can totally zap us of our energy and we become depressed and hopeless. Neither of these places is productive. The trick is to learn to harness the energy for the good. That is, learn how to channel it into action that will serve us and our grounded desires. **True power is using energy effectively to serve our grounded desires.**

Another characteristic of the power-sucking emotions is that when we are in them we completely lose the ability to "feel into" or understand the experiences of others. In terms of being effective, not being able to feel into the experience of others is a huge problem. If we cannot feel into the experiences of our children, we will be unable to work toward their best interests. When we are in the grip of power-sucking emotions we imagine that our view of reality is correct and that it will serve our children, but we are often wrong.

For instance, if we are angry at our ex, we may think that because she is not paying enough child support or isn't conscientious about making our children brush their teeth, she should have less time with our children. Unless our ex is truly abusive or neglectful, it is unlikely that our children would benefit from less time with their other parent. From the power-sucking emotions, we see things through our own lens only and imagine that what feels good to us would also be good for our children. If we look back at our grounded desires, we realize that we want our children to grow up to be happy and successful. If we are unable to feel into their experience, or more importantly feel things from their point of view, it is unlikely that we will be able to attain a grounded desire that is focused on their needs.

Fear is the driver

It is vitally important to realize that Power-Suckers are not **primary** emotions. They happen second. When somebody does something that triggers us, before we get angry, resentful, frustrated, exasperated or anxious, **we get SCARED. In other words, before we get angry, we have a fear reaction.** There are other ways to say this, and it is important to find the one that describes accurately what you feel:

1. I get scared.
2. I feel threatened.
3. I feel powerless.
4. I feel as though I am losing control.

Are you buying it? Most people don't at first. It can be difficult to recognize fear as it can quickly lead to another secondary emotion such as anger. Try thinking about it this way. When your ex says something like, "I'm going to court and getting custody of the kids," before you get angry, you get scared or feel threatened. You get scared that he might actually be able to carry out his threat. There is nothing more terrifying than the idea of losing your children.

If we think about it we will realize that everything that creates the Power-Sucker emotions is created by a fear reaction. Here is a list of basic fear thoughts that people in these difficult conflictual divorce situations may experience:

1. I'm afraid that I'll lose my kids.
2. I'm afraid I won't be able to support myself and my kids.
3. I'm afraid my ex won't give me the money I need to survive.
4. I'm afraid my ex will take all my money and I'll be left with nothing.
5. I'm afraid that my ex will cause my child/ren to be screwed up.
6. I'm afraid this situation will cause my child/ren to be screwed up.
7. I'm afraid that I'm screwed up and that's why this has all happened.
8. I'm afraid other people will see how screwed up I am.
9. Other people seem to know how to keep their lives in order, so I'm afraid there must be something wrong with me.
10. I'm afraid that my child/ren will wind up loving him/her more than they love me.
11. I'm afraid I'm a bad parent.
12. I'm afraid I'll be the "bad guy."
13. I'm afraid there is something wrong with me.
14. Because my child/ren will love my ex more than me, I'll wind up alone.
15. I'm afraid that my ex will convince my child/ren that I'm crazy or bad.

We **HATE** feeling fear. Fear makes us feel powerless, and we hate feeling powerless. We hate it so much that we immediately try to make ourselves not feel it. We attempt to not feel it by moving into a mode where we are either passively or actively trying to change our **external circumstances** so that we won't feel the fear anymore. When we are in the power-sucking emotions, we are feverishly trying to figure out how to change the **external circumstances** so that we won't feel the **FEAR** anymore.

Anger tends to be expressed in an active attempt to alter external circumstances--we yell or scheme at the external circumstances in order to make them change. When we are **frustrated** or **anxious** we repeatedly go over the facts trying to figure out how to change them. The problem with all of these is that they are almost always ineffective at getting us what we want. Occasionally, explosive anger will get us what we want in the short term, but it rarely if ever gets us what we want or need in the long run.

Facing fear

The reason we want to get ourselves free from the trap of the power-sucking emotions is because they **DO NOT WORK.** The doorway to getting out of them is to **get clear about what we are afraid of and really let ourselves feel the fear.** When we allow ourselves to feel fear, we can move through it and then decide what we are going to do about it once it has released its power over us. But if we do not recognize it first, it has much more power over us. By feeling it, looking at it, naming it and being aware of it, we diffuse its power.

The problem with not recognizing our fear is that we wind up acting out of it. In other words, even if we are not aware of it, it is what drives our action. **When we act out of fear, we wind up creating what we are afraid of.** How does that happen? Simple. When we act out of fear, we have no power, and when we have no power, we cannot create what we want, and when we cannot create what we want, we create the opposite—which is what we don't want.

Time and time again, I have seen people diffuse their power by getting angry in mediation or in court. For instance, if a woman's ex is making a case for how crazy she is, and then she acts crazy by allowing her anger, hatred or resentment (driven by fear) to dictate her actions, she winds up helping her ex make his case. Her fear of losing time with her children created the anger that made her look crazy, and may wind up actually contributing to her losing time with her children.

Our fears are connected to our deep desires. What we actually fear is that we will not get or have what we truly desire. At the heart of everything that we want, both for ourselves and our children, is to feel loved and secure. **But when we act out of fear, we diminish our ability to be loved and secure.**

Allowing fear leads to sadness

Recognizing our fear is the doorway through which we can work ourselves out of the power-sucking emotions. (See Figure 1) When we realize that fear is at the heart of our emotional reactivity, we gain the ability to look at the fear and work ourselves out of the reactive, power-sucking place. When we allow ourselves to feel and focus on the pure fear, an interesting thing happens. We get sad. When we are not running away from the fear, we can't help but look more clearly at the reality of our situation: we truly have, at least to some extent, lost some degree of control over the things that are most important to us. This is something to be sad about.

Sadness is another emotion that we like to avoid. It is painful. In our culture, we think that sadness is not OK. Crying is often thought of as a sign of weakness or self-indulgence. When we do not allow ourselves to feel it, it accumulates and grows and causes a big stuck place within us. The bigger it gets the more we want to avoid it, but the more we avoid it, the larger it looms in our unconscious. It keeps us from being flexible in the way we think about and react to things. Unlike the power-sucking emotions, sadness is grounded and real. When we allow ourselves to feel sad about the situation we are in and grieve our losses, our hearts are open, and our feet are on the ground. From this place we can think clearly and make decisions and take action that will be more effective. Sadness (or grief), if we allow ourselves to feel it, helps us get "unstuck."

Consider that when we allow ourselves to feel sadness and grief, we allow ourselves to let go of that stuckness within us. Letting go of it helps us to become more grounded and more flexible. Many of us avoid sadness and grief because we think that if we allow ourselves to feel it we will fall into an abyss or black hole that we will never be able to climb out of. Many people have told me that they fear that once they start crying they will never stop. This is not true. Think of it as a dam that needs to be released—even if you fear being overwhelmed by it, it is necessary to let it flow through you and out of you. You *will* stop crying, and you will feel better and be in a better place emotionally after you let it out.

In these exercises , you will work at learning to recognize your fear. In the next chapter, we will work with where to go from there.

Figure 1:
The Progression of an Emotional Reaction

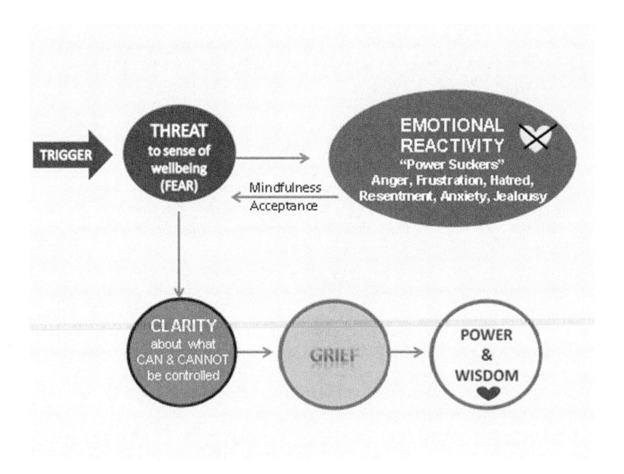

The pivotal point in this progression is being mindful of and accepting fear.

Exercises for Chapter 4

1. Name five things that you are afraid of concerning your divorced parenting situation.

2. Name two situations in which acting out of fear can result in creating what you are afraid of.

3. Throughout the course of your day, when you feel anger, frustration, resentment or anxiety, ask yourself what it is you are afraid of. Make a note of your discoveries.

4. When you let yourself fear, notice how it feels in your body-- where do you feel it, and what does it feel like. Describe the feeling that you notice.

Chapter 5
Know the Difference Between What You Can and Can't Control

*Grant me the serenity to accept the things I cannot change, courage
to change the things I can, and wisdom to know the difference.*
Reinhold Niebuhr

Imagine that we have a given amount of energy to expend in a day--let's say 1000 units of energy. Knowing that we have a finite amount, we would want to make sure we spend our precious units on actions to help ourselves move forward in our lives and help our children move forward in theirs. In other words, we would want to engage in actions that had value and effectiveness, actions that "packed a punch." Right?

To be sure we expend our energy on actions or thoughts that have value and will be effective, we have to look at what we do and do not have control over. If we continually put energy into what we cannot control, we waste precious energy. Even worse, it also keeps that energy from going into productive action. When it comes to acting in a way that will contribute to our own well-being and the well-being of our children, why would we want to waste that energy?

It is critical to recognize that we absolutely cannot control another person. We can INFLUENCE others, but we CANNOT CONTROL them. When it comes to our ex, we must accept that we cannot control her. We especially cannot control her if we are telling her or even just thinking about how bad and wrong she is , or if we are telling her or thinking about how she SHOULD be. Think about it. Do you respond well to someone who tells you that you are wrong or bad, or how you SHOULD be? Do you respond well to people who you know are thinking you are bad and wrong, even if they are not voicing it?

The Table
There is an exercise that I call "The Table." Go to a table in your home and look at it for a minute. Now, describe the table in terms of its physical attributes, such as, it is made of wood, it is square or rectangular, it is three feet high, etc. Now ask yourself what you would and wouldn't expect this table to do. For instance, you would expect this table to stay in the same place unless you move it, right? You would expect that if you put a plate on this table, the table would hold it up. But you would not expect the table to say "Good morning" to you and you would not expect the table to walk into another room.

You may laugh and say how silly, but what is really silly is that in spite of the fact that our ex has never behaved in some certain way, we continually expect her to behave in that certain way, and then get disappointed when she doesn't.

Example: Your ex has never been a good listener and does not try to understand your point of view. But, when you talk to him on the phone, you get upset and disappointed that he isn't listening and understanding your point of view.

Why do we expect people to do what they've never done? That's like looking at the table and being surprised when you say good morning to it and it doesn't say good morning back.

Letting go gains us power
When we accept what we cannot control, it may feel like losing power. But in reality, **we gain power, because we now have energy to expend on productive actions.**

For instance, a parent spends time on the phone with his ex engaged in an argument that goes nowhere. During this argument, the children are in the background, ignored and feeling the stress that this argument is creating. Even though this same parent has the grounded desire to raise a happy and fulfilled child, by engaging in this argument, the parent is working against his own grounded desires. If the parent accepted that fact he cannot change his ex and decided not to engage in the argument, instead turning his attention toward his children, he would be doing much more in the moment to contribute to his children's overall well-being and happiness.

"Energy Wasting Should Dance"
The fact that we cannot control people means that we cannot make them do what we think they SHOULD do. Let me introduce you to what I call the "Energy Wasting **Should** Dance." We humans have a lot of ideas about what others should and should not do. We say things like, "but my ex SHOULD pay more child support because it's the right thing to do. It's not OK that she doesn't do that! She SHOULD!" OK, maybe she should, but she doesn't and you can say that she should to yourself, to her, to your friends, to your child/ren, but repeating it over and over is not going to make her do it, so you are wasting your precious time and energy. If you are saying it over and over to people so that they will see how bad your ex is, you are also wasting your precious time and energy. Does it help anything for others to know how victimized you are or how wrong your ex is?

Be aware of the "Energy Wasting Should Dance." When you hear yourself using the S word, stop. Remind yourself that your ex is The Table, and that it doesn't matter what you think he should or should not do. Accept that he does exactly what he does, and ask yourself how you could better use your energy in this moment to achieve your deeply desired goals.

Acceptance and grief

The idea of accepting what we can and cannot control may seem simple, but it is not easy. We can have a difficult time accepting what we cannot control because it may mean accepting something that is very painful, or that we think may have a negative effect on our children. For instance, if you believe that our ex is mentally unstable, but the Court still grants her time with our children, it may be difficult to accept that we cannot control what happens when our children are with her, or the impact that our ex will have on our children over time.

Acceptance is often accompanied by sadness and grief. It makes us sad when we realize that we do not have control over the things that are nearest and dearest to us. It saddens us deeply when we realize that we cannot create the kinds of lives for our children that we imagined we would.

It is natural to try to turn away from grief, but ultimately, turning away from grief keeps us in a very stuck place. Allowing ourselves to feel and move through grief moves us toward a calmer, more grounded place. From this place we can make decisions that are smarter and work more effectively, toward achieving our grounded desires.

Exercises for Chapter 5

1. The Table Exercise: Just as with the table, describe your ex in terms of his or her attributes. For instance: My ex is kind to other people, but not to me. My ex lies. My ex is stingy with his money. My ex is a good father/mother. My ex is reliable. My ex is unreliable. Make this list a combination of positive and negative attributes if possible. Read the list out loud several times in a very neutral, unemotional way, as if you are describing the attributes of a table, and there is absolutely nothing emotional about it. Now, make a practice of noticing when you expect your ex to be other than how you know he or she is and rein yourself in!

2. A List of Shoulds: Make a list of all the things you think you ex should be doing, or ways that you think your ex should be that you ex is not. Notice throughout the course of the day how many times you either think about how your ex should be, tell other people how your ex should be, or think about or tell other people how your ex isn't what you think he or she should be. Notice when you say or think the "S" word, and turn yourself in another direction.

3. Ask yourself continually throughout the day whether you are engaging in an action or thought that will contribute positively to your life and the lives of your children. What actions and/or thoughts have you engaged in that contributed negatively and positively to your children's lives?

Chapter 6
Children Need to Know They are Loved, They Belong and They are Secure

You are the bows from which your children as living arrows are sent forth.
Khalil Gibran

In order to develop in a healthy way, children need to know they are loved, that they belong and that they are secure. Having parents that are divorced or separated or in the process **can** mess with their sense of being loved, their sense of belonging and their sense of security --**but it doesn't have to**. Children do not suffer as a result of divorce/separation because of the divorce or separation itself. **They suffer because parents think or behave in ways that diminish a child's sense of being loved, belonging and feeling secure.** This chapter will challenge you to explore the ways you may be doing this.

On a very basic level, children need to know that their world is a secure place, that it makes sense and that there are adults who care for them. We could look at it as though they develop a **story** or a **map of the world** that comes from their experiences. If they have a coherent story that fits together relatively well, they feel secure and they feel a sense of belonging. They do not have to waste energy wondering (consciously or unconsciously) whether they are secure; rather they can put their energy to growing, developing and experiencing the world.

What's your story?
Children get their stories or maps from things they learn from their parents. Parents in divorce situations usually have a story they tell about the divorce and why it happened. These stories usually involve some degree of blame. Often the blame focuses on what the other did or is doing wrong, or how the other parent is bad. Because the two parents often have very different stories, it is confusing to the child, especially if the two stories cannot both be true.

The stories that we believe about our divorces or about our ex seem as natural and true as the air we breathe. Parents often feel as though it is important for children to know the "truth." As much as we would like to believe there is a single accurate truth, there really isn't one. Every truth is subjective and multi-layered. We interpret the world through our individual lens, and our lens comes from our experiences and the beliefs that have either become instilled in us or that we developed on our own. We decide what the truth is by interpreting information through our unique lens.

Another person's truth can be very different than our own. As much as we love our own version of the truth, and want to believe it and have everyone else believe it, if we are going to walk down the very challenging path of evaluating ourselves so that we can be effective parents, we have to face the hard truth that **OUR** truth isn't necessarily **THE** truth. That doesn't mean that the other person's truth is the truth; it means that the truth is a very mushy thing.

The truth vs. your truth
Many parents believe adamantly and vehemently that children are entitled to **the truth.** If we find ourselves thinking that our children are entitled to the truth, we must challenge our own belief system. What we are really saying, if we are honest with ourselves, is that we want them to adopt **our truth**.

So what does this have to do with children feeling love, belonging and security? First, whether we like it or not, our ex is our child's parent. Parents are intensely and deeply important to children. We may be able to get over our ex, but our children cannot and in most cases will not and should not. When two parents have very different versions of the truth, it is very confusing for children whether they are 2 or 32. Even teenage or grown-up children who appear to be, or in actuality are adults, are still children when it comes to their parents and how they see them. Whether we think we should or not, they have loyalty to both parents. Trying to figure out how to reconcile two different versions of the story, and stay loyal to both parents, is extraordinarily hard on them.

When parents do not like each other and tell (either directly or subtly) two different versions of the truth, children do not know where they belong, and they feel insecure. Children feel on some level as though they are made up of each of their parents. When the two parents intensely dislike each other it is as if the child is made up of two parts that cannot get along. The battle will then become internalized, meaning that they do not know how to make peace with themselves on a psychological level.

This is a dilemma because we can't force ourselves to like our ex, and I'm not asking us to pretend like we do. In fact, we CAN'T pretend. Research shows that that only 7% of communication occurs through words, 38% occurs through how we vocalize (volume, pitch, rhythm, etc.) and a whopping 55% occurs through body movements, especially facial expressions. Therefore children will pick up our real feelings even if we don't verbally relate them. They pick up our feelings by how we talk (or don't talk) to our ex, how we talk about her, how we look at her, our non-verbal reactions when our children talk about her, etc. In addition, we say things when we don't think our children are listening, and they are (such as when we're on the phone in another room). So if we're thinking that we are very careful not to **say** things, we should think again. They are going to intuit our "story" whether we tell it to them or not.

Love in action
Let's talk a little about love. We all love our children, and I do not think we really have to go into the research that shows that loving children helps them be healthy. We know that down to our cells without any proof. But what the heck is love anyway? Scott Peck was a psychiatrist and best-selling author best known for his first book, _The Road Less Traveled_, published in 1978. He talks about love in this book: what it is, and what it isn't. He defines loves as "The will to extend

one's self for the purpose of nurturing one's own or another's spiritual growth." (In this context, spiritual can also mean emotional or psychological.) Love is primarily **actions** towards nurturing the spiritual growth of another. He says that love isn't feeling, it is action. We think that if we love someone, we are feeling all warm and fuzzy inside, but in reality love can be difficult and not feel good at all.

So, if we really love our children, in order to nurture their spiritual, emotional or psychological growth, we have to work toward giving them a coherent story that allows them to relax and focus on the business of being kids. Working on this story actually involves developing a clearer and more compassionate view of our ex. If we REALLY love our children, forget buying them things, taking them wonderful places and providing fun-filled experiences for them in hopes that will make up for the terrible feelings between us and our ex. None of that will compare to us stretching ourselves to find compassion for our ex so that we can help our children have a coherent, safe story about the world that contributes to them feeling loved and feeling a sense of belonging.

In asking us to find compassion for our ex, I am not asking us to give up, or allow us or our children to be treated neglectfully or badly. I am asking that we try to see our ex as a **distressed** person as opposed to a **bad** person. We will address how to begin doing that in the next chapter.

For now, it is important to begin looking at the story we have been telling ourselves, and what that means for our children. It is important to think about how we can rewrite our "divorce/separation story" in a way that is less blaming and more compassionate toward our ex. We can't dictate what story our ex tells, but we do have control over the one we tell. It will make a big difference, even if we are the only ones who do it.

Exercises for Chapter 6

1. What story do you tell about your divorce (either to yourself or others or both)? What part of this do you think would benefit your child/ren? Why would it benefit them? Think carefully and honestly about this.

2. Describe whether and how (either directly or indirectly) you tell your child/ren your version of the truth.

3. How do you imagine it feels to be a child who is being told (or picking up) two different stories? Write as if you are your child/ren about how it feels to have two different versions of the story.

Chapter 7
When People Behave Badly, They are Distressed

Hatred never ceases by hatred, but by love alone is healed.
This is an ancient and eternal law.
The Buddha

From Chapter 2, we know that when we get emotionally reactive, we are being driven by fear. Likewise, when our ex behaves badly we can assume that she is in a fear reaction. When I use the word fear, it can also refer to shame. The reason the word fear can be used to describe shame is that shame can be thought of as *the fear* that there is something essentially wrong with us. In fact, shame can be thought of as the deepest and most painful form of fear.

Human beings are very social and interdependent animals. As young children we can't physically survive on our own, and as adults we can't emotionally thrive on our own. Deep inside we need to believe that we fit in somewhere. We know that in order to fit in we must be essentially lovable and acceptable. If we don't think we are, we get scared that we will be alone. We have all known the experience of being worried that we will be rejected. These feelings often occur on an unconscious level. The idea that we are not good enough is so painful that it gets driven into our unconscious minds. In other words, we are not aware of feeling that way, but nonetheless, that feeling is driving our behavior.

Compass of Shame
Psychologist Donald Nathanson is an "affect theorist." (Affect is another word for emotion). He focuses a great deal of attention on shame because he believes it is so essential to our understanding of human beings, and human beings in relationship to each other. Nathanson talks about how shame is like a "spotlight" that focuses us on our "incapacity, deficit, failure; all kinds of things about our worst possible self." He says that shame feels terrible; in fact it is the most difficult affect to allow ourselves to feel. Therefore, he says, "Rather than maintain our attention on what feels awful to us, on our worst possible self, we learn from **our earliest childhood** a pattern of four styles of behavior, each of which reduces the likelihood that we're going to focus on what's wrong with us. I call this pattern of responses the Compass of Shame. We go into the Compass when we don't look at what the spotlight is showing us." (From an interview conducted with David Boulton in 2003 and published on "Children of the Code" website: www.childrenofthecode.org/interviews/nathanson.html)

The four styles of behavior on the Compass of Shame are: Withdrawal, Avoidance, Attack Others and Attack Self. We will talk about these patterns of behavior more in depth in the next chapter. But here's a brief introduction:

- **Withdrawal** refers to disconnecting and hiding ourselves from others.
- **Avoidance** refers to avoiding the feeling of shame by trying to make ourselves feel good in some other way, such as excelling at a sport or career. It can also refer to addiction or use of substances or activities to distract us from how we feel.
- **Attack Others** refers to how we lash out at others so as not to focus on ourselves and our fears about our inadequacies. When we fall into Attack Others, we create disconnection from the one we are attacking. People who can't tolerate the disconnection will fall into the Attack Self mode.
- **Attack Self** involves demeaning ourselves as a way of staying in relationship with the person who triggered our shame response.

In an earlier paragraph, I highlighted the part of Nathanson's quote that referred to how we learn these styles of behavior in our earliest childhoods. When people behave badly, they are often in a shame reaction, and are **reverting back to a very old and childlike form of behavior.** They learned this defensive behavior as a child when someone was being unkind to them or shaming them. Do you remember how you felt as a child when you were shamed? If you think of your ex as a confused and hurt child when she is behaving badly, you are likely to feel more compassion than if you are thinking of her as a mean or evil jerk who is just bad because somehow she enjoys being bad.

When people feel threatened, and fear that they are unlovable and bad, they tend to behave badly. Because these reactions occur at an unconscious level, they are not aware of the feelings of shame and fear. We can, however, bring it into consciousness for ourselves, and we can also cultivate compassion by realizing that when our ex behaves badly, he is suffering. Even if our ex does not realize this, it is helpful if we do, because it will help us feel less reactive and will also help us cultivate compassion.

Cultivate compassion

Cultivating compassion is very important. Most people in high-conflict divorced parenting situations cringe when asked to think about cultivating compassion for their ex. They believe deep down that their ex is not worthy of compassion. All humans are worthy of compassion and it actually benefits **us** to find compassion for our ex, maybe even more than it benefits them.

Finding compassion benefits us in three ways:

1. It helps our children, and of course, we are happy when we contribute to our children's wellbeing.
2. Compassion feels better than hatred.
3. We are much more grounded and powerful when we have compassion.

It will help our children because if we are feeling compassion we are not going to be hateful at the same time. Our children need us not to hate the other parent. Also, when we have compassion for the other parent, we are helping our children understand the other parent better, which helps our children be more psychologically healthy. And last, but certainly not least, we are modeling for our children how to be mature adults who are truly interested in living effective and satisfying lives. When we stay stuck in anger and resentment toward others we are unable to engage fully in our lives. We live in small psychological boxes and miss out on so much. Is that what we want to show our children? Is that really what we want for ourselves?

Now, let's get clear. Having compassion does not mean that we are going to lie down and give everything up or that we are going to be nice. It **simply** means that we **feel into another person's experience**. It means that we get a sense of what it is like to be that person. If we are able to realize that when the other person behaves badly he is distressed, shamed, feeling horrible underneath it all, we are going to be much more powerful than if we are seeing him as a mean bully. Mean bullies are intimidating; hurt children, not so much. We will be more powerful because seeing who he is deep down is much more accurate than seeing what is blurting out on the surface. We are going to understand the person much better, which will give us a better chance of effecting change.

A Story:

The Woman in My Seat

My ex-husband and his wife picked up the kids recently to take them on a two-week road trip. My sons were beaming with excitement as they loaded suitcases and backpacks into the car. "Did I pack my CD player?" my younger son yelled out to me. "Yes, you did, honey," I said, trying hard to hide the sadness that was coming over me in waves. The balloon of tears behind my eyes was growing and stretching thinner by the minute. I prayed it wouldn't explode until they could no longer see me waving good-bye in the rear view mirror.

If I hated road trips, this might be easier. But I love road trips. Memories of road trips with my children before the divorce flashed in front of me. I remembered one son peeing in a Coke bottle, and the rounds we'd sing as we went, "Don't put your dust in my dust pan, my dust pan, my dust pan. Fish and chips and vinegar, and pepper pepper pepper pop!" I remembered the euphoria I felt hitting the road with my ex on our first road trip, way before the kids were even a twinkle in my eye. There's nothing like new love and the open road to make the world feel like a wonderful place.

"We're set!" my ex shouted. Still lingering in memories, I headed toward the passenger door as if I was going on the trip. But wait a minute, there was a woman in my seat. The same eerie feeling I used to get when I watched The Twilight Zone rose up through my toes and landed queasily in the pit of stomach. It was as though I had gone to sleep and woken up in a different life. How did this woman replace me, become wife to my husband, mother to my children?

Breathing deeply, the feeling of strangeness was quickly replaced by another wave of sadness that settled in my heart and pressed firmly against my chest wall. Even though it was painful, I was grateful for the sadness. After all, until just recently, I was filled with anger toward this woman. Sadness is difficult, but anger is far worse. Sadness hurts, but it also heals, leaving in its wake a tender and open heart. Anger, on the other hand, feeds on itself, burning and destroying as it goes. Once it has you in its grip, anger doesn't want to let you go.

Believe me, I know. I held onto the anger at the woman in my seat for longer than I'd like to admit. I supposed if my ex had left me for her, my feelings would have seemed justified. But he didn't. Still, I clung to anger like a drowning man hangs onto a log bobbing in the ocean. I see now that it was easier to be angry than to face my own insecurities and the grief of a failed marriage. And who better to be angry with than this young and pretty addition to the family?

Bopping onto the scene several years ago, she was enthusiastic, eager, bubbly and fresh. I was threatened. Deep down, I was terrified that my children would trade in their old and boring mom, and go frolicking off into the sunset with the Supermom 2000 model - new and improved. She brought out my deepest, darkest insecurities. I became hardened and resentful.

I hated her for being nice to my kids. I hated her when I picked up my younger son, and he didn't want to leave her because they were laughing and eating popcorn together that she popped in a pot on the stove. I hated her because I saw my older son talking to her in an animated and smiley way only minutes after he had given me the cold shoulder. I hated her because she cheered enthusiastically at soccer games and insisted on going to school conferences.

Through the distorted lens of jealousy and insecurity, I saw her as a manipulative person who was trying to steal my kids away. It was especially hard at first, during their honeymoon period. She was working hard to make things work. They were going on outings, having family game nights, and generally having lots of fun. They bought a new home and were busy settling in. They were all excited and happy. When I would pick up the boys, I couldn't help but feel like I had dropped in on the stepfamily version of the Cleavers.

But honeymoons can only last so long, and it was when theirs ended that some drops of compassion started to seep into my bitter heart. My younger son, approaching adolescence, started being disrespectful to the woman in my seat. I remembered how my older son acted at that age. According to the stories I heard from my kids, she was handling the situation with my younger son the same way I handled it with my older son, very poorly. My heart ached for her for a moment. Having been through adolescence with one son, I had learned better ways to deal with it. Not having children of her own, she was as helpless as I had been the first time. I wouldn't wish that on anyone.

My frozen heart started to thaw slightly, but for the most part I kept my heels dug in. One day I was complaining to a friend about her. My friend shook her head and said, "Have a little pity for her. I wouldn't want you to be the mother of my stepchildren. You're a hard act to follow." Hearing those words made the world feel as though it had been out of focus and was suddenly becoming clear.

What was it like to be her? What was it like to walk into an existing family and make a place for yourself? What would it be like to establish yourself with children who already have a mother that they love? Finally, delayed though it was, it started dawning on me that she wasn't in an easy position. If I felt threatened, how could she possibly feel? What could it possibly be like to mother two kids who would never be hers?

Standing at the curb the day they left, I looked into the face of the woman in my seat. She looked different to me now, not the devious Cruella de Vil I once imagined her to be. She was a woman, like me, struggling to make a happy life for herself. She was a woman, like me, with strengths, weaknesses, successes and defeats. I reflected on our journey and knew that I'd come a long way. There was so much I had learned.

I learned that we are not in a competition. We can both have a relationship with the boys, and the quality of one will not detract from the quality of the other. I don't have to vie for their love as if there is a finite amount that will be split between us. In fact, ironically, I've learned that the more I accept and embrace her, the more my children will love me. Love creates love. I've also learned that nobody ever takes the place of Mom in a child's heart. When I remember that, I have compassion for the woman in my seat. As much as they love her, she will never be Mom.

When they pulled away, I cried many tears. I cried tears of grief for a mom, a dad and two kids who were once a family and were no more. I cried because when you divorce, your children have a life and family that doesn't include you. I cried because life often turns out so differently than you imagine it will. My deep sobs reminded me of the way my sons cried when they bumped their heads or skinned their knees. Just as their deep sobs eventually subsided into a relaxed contentment, so my crying finally dissolved into a profound feeling of peace.

It would be so easy to be bitter. How well I know that. But this is our life now. Every decision, every turn in life, every change, has its sadness. There is nothing to be mad about. Imagining them driving down the highway, I hoped that their trip would be safe and happy. I hoped that the woman in the front passenger seat, HER seat, would bring my children some joy, and that they would return it. I hoped that my ex would be peaceful and relaxed. I hoped they would sing lots of songs, laugh and kid, and remember to always have an empty Coke bottle for those times when gas stations are few and far between.

Exercises for Chapter 7

1. Make a list of ways that you think your ex may be feeling shame or insecurity.

2. Consider the fact that there are things about you that make your ex feel powerless or insecure. What might those things be?

3. Make a list of ways that cultivating compassion will help your children.

Chapter 8
Patterns are Powerful

All fixed set patterns are incapable of adaptability or pliability.
The truth is outside of all fixed patterns.
Bruce Lee

The way we react to others, especially when we are in an emotionally reactive state, comes largely from strategies and patterns that became deeply ingrained in us when we were young. When we are acting out of emotional reactivity, we tend to fall unconsciously into our old patterns. In the previous chapter I talked about how Donald Nathanson, the affect theorist, describes the styles of behavior we fall back on when we are trying to avoid shame. Another way to look at this -- and the way I am going to talk about it here - is as the strategy people use when they feel powerless. When two people are in conflict, they are each in their own shame/fear reaction. In other words, they feel powerless, and they fall back into a patterned way of responding. The way they respond to each other becomes repetitive and unproductive. You can call this repetitive way of relating a "dynamic" or a "pattern."

Be conscious of the dynamic
It is very important to recognize and get conscious about how this dynamic works in order to have the power to rise above it and learn to operate in a way that is more effective. It is also very important to acknowledge our part in the dynamic. What do we do that gets the dynamic going, or keeps the dynamic going? We may feel as though we **just respond** to what the other person hurls at us. Be aware that even if we feel like we are just responding, the way we respond is **part of the dynamic,** and we do have control over that. When we are in conflict we often feel victimized by the other, as if we have no power and no control over the situation. This is not true! We do have the power to change the way we participate in the dynamic, even if we cannot change the way our ex engages in the dynamic.

Let's look again at the four strategies described in the previous chapter: Attack Others, Attack Self, Withdrawal, Avoidance. Although we may use a combination of strategies, often we fall into one or two more than the others. The way I think about it is that when we feel threatened in some way, if we are not being conscious, we retreat to one of these strategies. It is important to get clear about what these strategies look like so we can recognize them in ourselves and in our ex.

Attack Others is blaming the other. In this strategy, we believe that the other is causing our difficulties, and that if they would just change, everything would be all right. We think we have to work hard at making them change and that we will gain power by changing them.

Attack Self involves demeaning ourselves, or taking the blame onto ourselves, past the point of reasonableness. It is important to take responsibility for ourselves, but this goes beyond that.

The idea is that we feel as though the only way to have some power is to belittle ourselves.

Withdrawal involves running away or hiding, either in reality or emotionally. When we are in withdrawal we are hard to communicate with. In this strategy, we protect ourselves from the feeling of powerlessness by not engaging in the things that make us feel powerless.

Avoidance involves distracting ourselves with addictive substances or behaviors, or "puffing ourselves up" so that the feeling of shame is avoided. By puffing up, I mean making ourselves feel competent or superior in some way, so that we don't feel incompetent or powerless in another area.

When it comes to dynamics, we look at what strategy each of the people in the dynamic falls back to and how they interact with each other. In high-conflict divorce situations, at least one person usually falls back to the Attack Other strategy. Without at least one person in that mode, there wouldn't be conflict. (Of course, combinations of the other strategies can be problematic in other ways, but generally those are not what we are dealing with here.) Here are some common dynamic combinations in high conflict divorce situations.

Attack Other → ←Attack Other (Both people are blaming the other)
Attack Other →→ Withdrawal (One person is blaming and one person is withdrawing)
Attack Other →→ Avoidance (One person is blaming and one person is avoiding)

Can you identify which pattern tends to fit you and your ex? Imagine you are looking at this dynamic as if you are not part of it-- as if you're standing outside of it and seeing it from afar. What does it look like from far away or from up above or from the outside? If you were watching other people in this dynamic, what would you say about it? What would you tell them to do differently?

Now remember, we enter the dynamic the way we do because we feel threatened or powerless. What if we felt powerful? What would we do differently? Remember, we cannot change the way the other person enters the dynamic-- we can only change the way we enter it.

How can we change it?
Here are some ways we can change the way we enter the dynamic depending on what strategy you're in.

Attack Other: The characteristic of this strategy is to believe that it is the other person's fault and that in order to feel powerful, you will have to change her. Remind yourself that you cannot change her and that whatever you're doing at the moment that you believe is going to affect change is not going to work. If you are telling her what she is doing wrong, stop. It will not work.

Withdrawal: Notice that you are avoiding dealing with the situation at hand. Think about what you are afraid of and how you feel threatened. Remind yourself that by withdrawing, you contribute to a dynamic in which your ex will continue blaming and attacking. The more you withdraw, the more your ex will come toward you. If you can keep yourself from withdrawing, it will probably help your ex reduce the blaming.

Avoidance: The characteristic of this strategy is to avoid the feeling of powerlessness by making yourself feel powerful in other ways, or using substances or behaviors to distract yourself away from the feelings of powerlessness. Most likely you are avoiding your ex in some way which, as in withdrawal, just makes them come toward you more.

Here's the bad news: it is very difficult to change the way we enter the dynamic because it's our "default" mode. It's what we've always done, and what we're used to. It feels strange and even wrong to do it differently. It takes work. It takes consciousness. It takes sitting with some very difficult feelings. The reason we go to our default mode is because we are trying to avoid the feelings of powerlessness, and if we do not go to the default mode, we have to feel our feelings of powerlessness.

But that is exactly what we do, because when we allow ourselves to feel the fear, shame and powerlessness, we will drop into the sadness or grief. Remember that these emotions are more grounded. Once we're more grounded, we can begin to think of other ways to go about doing what we need to do in order to accomplish what we want to accomplish.

Exercises for Chapter 8

1. Describe the dynamic that you have with your ex.

2. Describe the way you enter the dynamic.

3. Describe ways that you can avoid entering the dynamic this way.

Chapter 9
We Create What We Focus On

What you love you empower,
And what you fear you empower-
And what you empower you attract.
Unknown

We can change our world by changing what we focus on. In divorced co-parenting situations, fear can cause us to focus on what is wrong. Focusing on what is wrong tends to create more of what is wrong. I am not suggesting that we go into denial or ignore what needs attention. I am suggesting that we consider how much attention we give negative ideas, and consider whether it is possible to shift toward more positive ideas.

Rick Hanson, a well-known neuropsychologist talks about how our brains have a negativity bias. He explains that "your brain preferentially scans for, registers, stores, recalls, and reacts to unpleasant experiences....it's like Velcro for negative experiences and Teflon for positive ones. Consequently, even when positive experiences outnumber negative ones, the pile of negative implicit memories naturally grows faster. Then the background feeling of what it feels like to be you can become undeservedly glum and pessimistic." (Hanson, Rick (2009-11-01). Buddha's Brain: The Practical Neuroscience of Happiness, Love, and Wisdom (p. 68). New Harbinger Publications, Inc. Kindle Edition)

Taking in the good
To counteract this negativity bias, Dr. Hanson developed a technique he calls "Taking in the Good." In "Buddha's Brain" (previously noted) he states: "The remedy is not to suppress negative experiences; when they happen, they happen. Rather, it is to foster positive experiences— and in particular, to take them in so they become a permanent part of you." His technique for "taking in the good" focuses on noticing positive experiences, allowing ourselves to more fully feel positive experiences and to focus on allowing the experiences to actually become part of us.

Children benefit when we focus on what's right about our lives and their lives. It is easy to realize what is good if we consciously turn our focus toward it. We cannot choose the experiences that we have had, or some of the facts about our lives, but we can choose what we focus on.

Gratitude transforms
Gratitude is powerful for turning us toward what is positive. Give the following exercise a try. You can do it alone, but doing it with another person is better. You can even do it with your child/ren. Set a timer for 10 minutes. Name as many things as you can that you are grateful for.

If you are doing it with another person, alternate saying the things you are grateful for. The things you name don't have to be big. They can be small and they can be things that we take for granted.

Here are some examples:
I am grateful that I have indoor plumbing.
I am grateful that it was a sunny day.
I am grateful that I have a home to live in.
I am grateful that I have a car to transport me.
I am grateful for microwave popcorn.
I am grateful that I have two healthy children.
I am grateful that I have a comfortable bed to sleep in.
I am grateful that I have a job.
I am grateful that I have grocery stores to shop at that have a wide variety of items.
I am grateful that I have good friends.
I am grateful I felt good today.

Notice how you feel after ten minutes of engaging in this exercise. Now, if you had done the same thing, only concentrated on what was negative, how do you imagine you'd feel? Are the negative things any truer than the positive things?

What we focus on determines how we feel. What we focus on and how we feel determines what our children focus on and what they feel. If we can cultivate a practice of turning toward what's good, and being grateful for the many positive things in our lives, our children will benefit immensely.

Exercises for Chapter 9

1. Write a list of 30 things that you are grateful for.

2. Think of one thing that is very positive about your child/ren's live. Spend ten minutes focusing on this positive thing. Let yourself take in how good it feels to think of this positive thing. Describe this experience.

3. At your next meal with your child/ren engage them in the gratitude exercise. Notice their emotional response and your emotional response. Describe it here.

Conclusion

Does this path have a heart? If it does, the path is good; if it doesn't, it is of no use.
Carlos Castaneda

You are at a turning point in your life. You are creating the rest of your life for you and your children. Remember what it is you want to create, and be wise about how you create it. Stay focused on your grounded desires. You have the power to guide your own journey.

Stay attuned to your child/ren. Listen to the deeper truth underneath their words. Remember what they really need.

Don't be afraid of fear. Let yourself feel it. If you don't turn from it, you will be led to a place of wisdom.

Let go of what you can't control. Let yourself grieve the loss of what you thought you could control but can't. Grieve the loss of how you thought your life would be but isn't.

Do the hard work of finding compassion for your ex. It will transform you, and will benefit your child/ren in ways that you can't even imagine.

Focus on what's positive. You will be amazed how much there is to be grateful for!

Stay focused on your heart. Your heart knows what to do. Take time to listen to it.

Thank you for your kind attention, and have a joyful and fruitful journey!

Printed in Great Britain
by Amazon

62622856R00045